# *the* TEN COMMANDMENTS *for* BUSINESS

*Biblical Truths for Eternally-Minded Entrepreneurs*

# *the* TEN COMMANDMENTS *for* BUSINESS

*Biblical Truths for Eternally-Minded Entrepreneurs*

*by Adam R. Hall, CPA, CGMA*

THE WORD ON BUSINESS™
BIBLICAL WISDOM FOR MAXIMUM SUCCESS

TheWordonBusiness.com

First Printing: May 2018



The Word on Business, Inc
7233 Clinton Road, Suite 201
P.O. Box 428
Stedman, NC 28391
(910) 758-1484
support@thewordonbusiness.com
TheWordonBusiness.com

Cover Design and Typography by Justin Turley

All Scripture is from the English Standard Version (ESV), unless otherwise stated.

Printed in the United States of America.

ISBN 978-0-692-09167-8

# TABLE *of* CONTENTS

# Acknowledgments

Thank you to my daughter, Alyssa Hall, for helping me write much of this book. Without her, this project would have never been completed. Also, thank you to my wife, Terrah, for the prayers, support, and encouragement that she generously gives to me each day. Finally, thank you to my parents for drilling the Word of God deeply into me and demonstrating to me that the Bible contains all we need to know for life and business.

# INTRODUCTION

When you want to maximize your business, to what resources do you turn for counsel? You might seek out a trusted friend or advisor, you might read best-selling business literature, or you might even pay a consultant to help you sort through complicated situations. While there is nothing wrong with pursuing those options, it must be clearly understood that all of the wisdom necessary for maximizing your business can be found within the pages of the Bible. Sadly, many Christian-owned businesses suffer as believers fail to seek out biblical wisdom for use in business management and they neglect to apply that scriptural wisdom to the everyday operations of their businesses. My hope is that as you examine the Ten Commandments with a business application focus, the Lord will give you fresh inspiration and insight for your business. It is my desire that you will come to believe wholeheartedly that Scripture is—and will always be—the best source of counsel for business. Its truths are timeless and its wisdom is matchless.

The Bible is widely recognized as the best selling and most widely distributed book (Guinness World Records). A survey by the Bible Society concluded that around 2.5 billion copies were printed between 1815 and 1975, but more recent estimates put the number at more than 5 billion. The whole Bible has been translated into 349 languages; 2,123 languages have at least one book of the Bible in that language. Why has the Bible managed to remain the most prominent, most widely disseminated book of all time? It's because the truth of God's Word endures forever and it alone can provide the wisdom and light that our souls crave. The Bible, and the wisdom contained therein, are timeless. It is rife with wisdom and application for all areas of life, not least of all in the business world.

In this book, we will interpret the Ten Commandments, found in Exodus 20:1-17, through the perspective of a small business owner. We will demonstrate how the principles within each of the commandments can be applied to your business. You will not only discover what each of the commandments mean—you will also gain some practical considerations for application to help you make changes in your business right now to more align yourself and your enterprise with the truth of Scripture.

Additionally, we have included a bonus discussion at the end of this book dealing with the issue of debt, as addressed in Proverbs 22:7. While this verse is obviously not one of the Ten Commandments, the truth it imparts is so relevant and applicable for business owners that we have decided to include it here, for the maximum benefit of the reader.

As a final word for this introduction, I do realize that throughout this book, there are some hard truths that have been expounded with a corresponding level of gravity. I have included the difficult truths of Scripture because I feel obligated to the Lord to speak His truth as honestly and completely as I can, not because I am someone who has arrived at any level of spiritual supremacy. Quite on the contrary, I felt a good deal of conviction while writing this book. I find myself daily confronted by my own weaknesses, and like every believer on this side of heaven, I still do battle with the world, the flesh, and the Devil each day in order to honor God with my life and my business. So please understand that I write these difficult things with the heart of a humble brother, not of a whitewashed Pharisee.

May God bless you as you seek to know His Word so that by it, you may honor and glorify Him in your life and your business!

---

For more resources, including The Word on Business Inner-Circle membership, books, online courses, a community forum, and more, visit our website today at TheWordonBusiness.com. We look forward to serving you!

COMMANDMENTS 1 & 2

# NO OTHER GODS *and* NO IDOLS

*"You shall have no other gods before me. You shall not make for yourself a carved image, or any likeness of anything that is in heaven above, or that is in the earth beneath, or that is in the water under the earth. You shall not bow down to them or serve them, for I the Lord your God am a jealous God, visiting the iniquity of the fathers on the children to the third and the fourth generation of those who hate me, but showing steadfast love to thousands of those who love me and keep my commandments." —Exodus 20:3-6*

What makes something your god? At what point does a passion that enriches your life cross the line to become an idol? At what point does an excitement about running your business edge out the Creator as supreme ruler of your heart? When exactly does a love for your business, your family, your recreation, or any other thing become first in your affections, even over a love for God?

The line between each of these things is not always as clear as it may seem. Beware of the trap of holding God dearly, *but* on the same plane as your friends, your family, or your beloved activities. Until and unless you can say with the Psalmist, "Whom have I in heaven but you? And there is nothing on earth that I desire besides you," then you may be harboring idols in your heart (Psalm 73:25). If the undergirding motivations for everything that you do in life are to satisfy wants that are not a longing for closeness with God and for His will to be done, then something has taken first place in your heart and it must be removed. In short, nothing must be more precious to you than your relationship with your Redeemer and the advancement of His kingdom and His will. Until He is all our hope, our love, our longing, our delight, our portion, our treasure (Matthew 6:19-21), then something is out of place.

In attempting to understand this commandment, it is often easy to view this mandate from God as being petty and prideful, demanding that He be the most important thing to us for the sake of exerting dictatorial control. Upon deeper consideration however, it becomes apparent that He commands this absolute level of commitment for at least one very good reason. He commands that we worship Him alone because it is the way things were created to be in the very beginning. From the dawn of humanity, God created men and women to love Him first and best. When we are doing this, we are functioning in accordance with our God-given design and purpose. As a result, worshipping God alone is actually what is *best* for us: making us the most satisfied, most fulfilled, and most joyful people possible when we are living in obedience to Him in this respect.

In my personal experience as a CPA in public practice, I've witnessed many Christian business owners make gods for themselves; idols out of their businesses.

Exodus 20:3 tells us that we must have no other gods before the one true God. It is important to ask yourself, have *you* put your business before God? Business owners are easily consumed with customer and client demands, employee drama, and financial concerns, all vying for their highest level of attention and priority. If we are not careful, at some point, our morning productivity can become more important to us than our morning devotion or prayer time. Our minds and thoughts can easily be dominated by all the demands of being a business owner. It seems someone or something is always competing for our attention, and it can be difficult to keep the best part of our focus centered on God.

Most business owners are driven by a desire to serve others, which is truly a great and noble thing. However, difficulty arises when the desire to serve your business supersedes your desire to serve God. Regarding idols in Exodus 20:4, Scripture instructs that we are not to "bow down to them or serve them." How can a person tell whether he or she has crossed the line from serving the Lord, to serving his or her business first and foremost? This question can be very personal and there is not an exact formula to determine when a person has crossed the line from merely being industrious to worshipping their business. Listed below, however, are some symptoms that exist when a business has become a god or an idol that may be helpful in determining one's level of commitment to business rather than to God.

- Your first thoughts upon waking in the morning are about business.
- Your last thoughts in the evening are about business.
- Most of the thoughts you have in your free moments are concerning business.
- Almost all your conversations are either dominated by business or at least always get tied back to it in some way.
- Business frequently interferes with church attendance, family functions, vacations, and other important events.
- Business precludes you from participating in other service opportunities.
- Business demands have crowded out time for Scripture study, meditation and prayer.
- You use more creative thought for making profit than for making disciples.

Do any of the symptoms listed above reflect the reality of your life? If only a few of these symptoms apply, then maybe you just need to balance a few things. However, if most of these symptoms apply to you, then consider bowing before the Lord in repentance and committing to put Him first before **all** things in your life, including your business.

During my first years as a young business owner, I was guilty of every symptom that I've listed here. The Lord blessed me with a business, and then I allowed it to consume me and eventually crowd out everything in my life, including God Himself. Thankfully, the Lord humbled me, and I was able to repent of my sins and experience freedom and restoration by allowing the Lord to dominate my life and business. After all, the Lord did not bless me with a business so that I would be devoted to it rather than to Him.

So consider what excites you, what drives you, what you long for, and then see if those things are coming from a heart that has put God absolutely first, or if they are springing from a spirit of carnality that is in need of reorientation, such as I had? Be honest with yourself, but in your assessment, don't forget that God is ever-gracious and patient with our constant failures and that none of our mistakes are unknown to Him. He, like the father in the parable of the prodigal son in Luke 15, opens His arms wide to welcome His sons and daughters who have strayed.

Isaiah 48:17 says: "Thus says the Lord, your Redeemer, the Holy One of Israel 'I am the Lord your God, who teaches you to profit, who leads you in the way you should go.'" It is God who lends us the health and presence of mind to run a business at all. Let Him be the most important thing in your life, always.

TAKE AWAY

- God, your Creator and Savior, should always be your first priority. Not merely a high priority, but **first** priority.
- Your business, or anything that dominates your thoughts and motivations, may be a god or an idol for you.
- Your business is a gift from God, not an idol to be served in place of Him.

COMMANDMENT 3

# YOU SHALL NOT MISUSE GOD'S NAME

*"You shall not take the name of the Lord your God in vain, for the Lord will not hold him guiltless who takes his name in vain. —Exodus 20:7*

Did you know that God's name, *YHWH*, is considered so holy by the Jews that they refuse either to speak or spell it, instead referring to Him in writing as G-d, and using the familiar form, *Adonai*, in their speech (Erlick, 2017)? Throughout the ages, the Jews have so revered God that they dared not even come close to transgressing this commandment, instead creating hedges, such as the one described above, to keep them from the slightest misuse of His precious name (Erlick, 2017). Sadly, one can hear many a professing Christian use either God's name itself, or some variant of it, to express feelings of excitement, anger, disbelief, or almost any other emotion, and such diction is widely accepted by Christian business owners who justify the practice, arguing that using God's name in that way is simply employing vernacular language that everyone understands.

Because we hear God's name so frequently misused, whether we are at work, talking to friends, enjoying a hobby with others, or even watching television, we have to ask ourselves, why is taking the Lord's name in vain such a weighty offense? We can think of it this way: God's name refers to the most powerful and preeminent Being who has ever existed or who will ever exist, who, by His own power and wisdom, created the universe and our own planet, and everyone and everything contained in it. A certain sense of healthy fear should fall upon each of us as we consider the might and power of God. Yet, when we use His name flippantly, we not only offend God, but we also convey to the world that He is not to be revered or respected, even that He is not a being at all. Especially if you are a known Christian, this practice can absolutely destroy any witness that you or your business might have.

By way of example, I once walked up on a friend of mine just as he was wrapping up a phone call with one of his customers. In the few minutes of conversation that I caught, I heard language from his mouth that I would never have expected to be uttered from this friend. When I confronted him about it, he quickly justified his language by excusing it as simply being part of running a business. However, the thought occurred to me afterward that my friend will never have the clout or opportunity to invite that customer to church or share the Gospel with him after speaking to him with such profane language.

God does not expect us to be completely perfect, but He has called us to pursue righteousness, as 1 Peter 1:16 instructs, "You shall be holy, for I am holy." Maintaining purity of speech protects our Christian witness, it separates us from the world, and it helps to open the door to sharing Christ with others. We cannot swear with the Lord's name in one sentence and then share the Gospel in the next breath and honestly expect others to heed our message. Our hypocrisy in this way would simply belie the fact that we do not reverence God ourselves.

The world has made such common use of God's name in swearing that it is astonishingly easy to become desensitized to its misuse. Let us not be conformed to the world's use of the name of God. Instead, let us hold the name of our God, including the terms "Lord," "Christ," and "Jesus" in such high esteem that we only use those names reverently, carefully, and purposefully.

While taking the Lord's name in vain includes, of course, the wrongful use of God's name in our speech, transgression of this commandment actually goes beyond mere semantics. Matthew Henry, the distinguished Bible commentator, explains that the Lord's name can be taken in vain in the follow manner:

> *"By hypocrisy, making a profession of God's name, but not living up to that profession. Those that name the name of Christ, but do not depart from iniquity, as that name binds them to do, name it in vain; their worship is vain (Matthew 15:7-9), their oblations are vain (Isaiah 1:11, 13), their religion is vain (James 1:26)."*

If we claim the name of Christ publicly, and yet live in such a way that misrepresents God's nature or character by leading a lifestyle of unconfessed and unrepentant sin, we are defaming God's name and will not be held guiltless, according to Exodus 20:7. As business owners, we each occupy a position of influence and visibility that can serve either as a beacon from which our light can shine to the world, or as a stage for our blatant hypocrisy to publicly smear God's name, and repel the lost from Him, rather than drawing them nearer to Him.

There was once a businessman in my community who was well-known for his public profession of faith in Christ and the fact that he often spoke of the Lord as the object of his praise and affection. From the outside, this man appeared to be a strong and outspoken Christian of the most spiritual sort. Regrettably, among those who did business with this man, he was known to be someone who relied upon unscrupulous business strategies, such as routinely writing bad checks and engaging in objectionable schemes. Many times throughout the years, I have heard others express their frustration with the irreconcilable gulf between this man's words, and his dishonorable actions. As a matter of fact, several individuals have expressed that his presence at the local church he attended was enough to keep them from going there themselves. His hypocrisy was so toxic to them that they could not stand to be in fellowship with him.

As a business owner, you will have the opportunity to bear the name of Christ to many people in this lost and broken world; in fact, for some, you may be the only link to Christ that they ever know. The way you represent the Lord to them can either accurately reflect the righteous character of Christ, or it can demonstrate falsely to them that to be a Christian means nothing more than to engage in the same sins that characterize the basest of the unsaved. If we take upon ourselves to profess the name of Christ with our mouths, we ought to make very sure that the way we treat everyone with whom we come into contact represents Christ in the best and most veritable way possible. When we invoke the name of Christ publicly and yet persist in unrighteous living, we not only put our Christian witness on the chopping block—we may also be making ourselves a barrier that hinders others from coming to Christ.

As we strive to honor God's name, please understand that complete perfection is not the expectation here. We each stumble in many ways as we try our hardest to follow Christ, and we could each be labeled a hypocrite at some time or another. However, our *reputation* ought to be as someone whose actions routinely reflect the righteousness and goodness of the Lord, rather than as a crook or a charlatan.

With this understanding, let us examine our speech, specifically our use of God's name, as well as our life and actions to ensure that we glorify the Lord at all times, as Psalm 34:1 reads: "I will bless the Lord at all times; his praise shall continually be in my mouth."

TAKE AWAY

- All names for God should be used with reverence, humility, respect and purpose.
- Protect your Christian witness in the eyes of your business associates by using God's name properly.
- Do not allow yourself to become desensitized to the misuse of God's name.
- Make every effort to ensure that the way you run your business accurately reflects the righteous character of the God you exalt with your words.

COMMANDMENT 4

# KEEP *the* SABBATH DAY HOLY

*"Remember the Sabbath day, to keep it holy. Six days you shall labor, and do all your work, but the seventh day is a Sabbath to the Lord your God. On it you shall not do any work, you, or your son, or your daughter, your male servant, or your female servant, or your livestock, or the sojourner who is within your gates. For in six days the Lord made heaven and earth, the sea, and all that is in them, and rested on the seventh day. Therefore the Lord blessed the Sabbath day and made it holy." —Exodus 20:8-11*

These days, keeping the Sabbath often seems more like a tradition or a suggestion rather than a commandment, but did you know that God actually takes the breaking of the Sabbath extremely seriously? Exodus 31:14 states, "You shall keep the Sabbath, because it is holy for you. *Everyone who profanes it shall be put to death*" (italics added). Additionally, He cites Sabbath-breaking as a prominent reason for His judgment of Israel in Ezekiel 20 and 22, "But the house of Israel rebelled against me in the wilderness…and my Sabbaths they greatly profaned. Then I said I would pour out my wrath upon them in the wilderness, *to make a full end of them*" (Ezekiel 20:13, italics added). Hearing language like this should definitely cause us to reconsider how we keep the Sabbath.

Perhaps, like many of us, you are unsure as to what exactly is expected of Christians on the Sabbath day. You know that going to church is definitely a priority and that you really shouldn't work on those days, but is there anything else that you should avoid, or perhaps that you should actually seek to *do* on the Sabbath?

Let's take a look at how the Bible handles the issue of keeping the Sabbath. The Scripture says that on the Sabbath "…you shall not do any work." For clarification, "work" in this context appears to be the earning of a livelihood that can be put off until the next day. This is an important point to understand. Suppose you have a medical practice which necessarily has "on call" weekends where you and your employees must attend to patients. According to this understanding of what qualifies as "work," your business is not breaking the Sabbath. Growing up, my father was a farmer and it was always his priority to avoid doing farm work on Sundays. However, if there were issues that could not wait until Monday—suppose, for example, that one of our calves needed medical care—we would certainly do what needed to be done. Harvesting grain and other similar tasks could of course wait until Monday, and were always put off until the Sabbath had ended.

You might be asking what it means for you and your business to "not do any work" on the Sabbath. The answer to this question depends greatly on what type of business you operate. Let's consider some Scripture from Matthew 12 to help us understand.

For a bit of context, the Pharisees in this passage, in an attempt to avoid breaking the fourth commandment, had actually created a long list of legalisms to be kept on the Sabbath that had not been commanded by God in His Law. In response to this asceticism, Jesus told them,

"The Son of Man is lord of the Sabbath," meaning that it is ultimately more important to love and honor Him than it is to immaculately observe man-made Sabbath-keeping parameters (Matthew 12:8). A bit later in the same chapter, the Pharisees were criticizing Jesus for healing a man with a withered hand on the Sabbath day, to which He gave them this reply, "Which one of you who has a sheep, if it falls into a pit on the Sabbath, will not take hold of it and lift it out? Of how much more value is a man than a sheep! *So it is lawful to do good on the Sabbath*" (Matthew 12:11-12, italics added). Jesus' comments here seem to indicate that—contrary to the Pharisaical view of keeping the Sabbath, which was based upon refraining from most activity—the Sabbath can be kept while remaining busy doing good. This means that when you are operating within the will of God, including caring for the needs of others, you are not breaking the Sabbath—you are actually honoring God.

With this principle in mind, it seems apparent that work performed on Sunday that meets a critical, timely need—that of health care professionals, for example—is not a violation of the Sabbath and is, in fact a mercy. However, if your business serves needs for your customers that are optional in timing (specifically, not threatening to a person's health or well-being if delayed), then the scriptural principle of not doing any work absolutely applies. I have owned an accounting practice for decades, and I've never encountered an accounting emergency that could not be suspended for one day. Even during our busy season, we refuse to work on Sundays as a result of our commitment to keeping this commandment and enjoying the rest it is designed to provide.

Let's take a minute to observe the Sabbath-keeping practices of a couple of large businesses. In the food service and retail space, Chick-fil-A and Hobby Lobby have both decided not to be open on Sundays and, as of today, their businesses are operating very profitably. In fact, despite being closed one day a week, Chick-fil-A is **the** highest-grossing-per-store fast food restaurant in the US (Peterson, 2017). In the Christian bookstore space, Lifeway, which is closed on Sundays, is operating profitably. In contrast, its direct competitor, Family Christian Stores, closed in 2017 after 85 years of operation. At the time of its closing, they had over 3000 employees in 240 stores across 36 states. Unlike Lifeway, they had chosen to be open on Sundays.

While I am not suggesting that their decision to be open on Sundays was the only reason they closed, we do know that God consistently honors those who walk in obedience to Him and often will withhold blessing from those who walk in opposition to His laws.

If your business has a choice, choose to be closed on Sunday. If, however, your business is in a position to "do good" on Sunday out of necessity, then so be it. Only be sure that your decision to be open at those times is entirely for the benefit of those with a critical need, not solely for profit.

As a great example of "doing good" on the Sabbath, Chick-fil-A did actually do work on a Sunday in Atlanta after a power outage stranded passengers at the world's biggest airport on December 17, 2017. However, they were not selling food; instead they opened their kitchens to cook and give away over 5,000 sandwiches to stranded passengers (Bartiromo, 2017). Such actions demonstrate the difference between doing work and doing *good*.

For most business owners, breaking or keeping the Sabbath is a matter of choice. Will you choose to worship and rest, or will you choose to try to get ahead by doing some extra business-related work that you didn't finish in the other six days of the week? We can be sure that we are never getting ahead if we are going against Scripture. That said, it is dangerous to create legalisms that determine what work "can wait" and what work "cannot wait" until Monday. If we will each diligently and humbly seek God's will for our lives and our businesses in that regard, we will be able to make the right decision that best allows us to honor God with the first fruits of our time, and yet allows us to meet the critical needs of others.

While we are deciding what it should look like in our lives and our businesses to keep the Sabbath, we might ask, "*Why* does God give us the Sabbath and require us to keep it?" From examining Scripture, there appear to be several reasons for this. Most obviously, Genesis 2:1-3 says:

> *"Thus the heavens and the earth were finished, and all the host of them. And on the seventh day God finished his work that he had done, and he rested on the seventh day from all his work that he had done. So God blessed the seventh day and made it holy, because on it God rested from all his work that he had done in creation."*

The Sabbath, it seems, was instituted to be a day for us to remember God's creating work and to enjoy rest and communion with Him. God, of course, is a spirit, and as such, does not deal with the frailties of humanity that we experience, such as physical exhaustion. Yet, in His wisdom, He ordained a day for us not only to find restoration for our physical bodies, but also to find spiritual nourishment as we turn our hearts and minds toward our Creator. To neglect the keeping of this special time is not only to experience physical, mental, and emotional burnout, but also to starve oneself spiritually, all of which can spell disaster for your business. If, however, you set aside the Sabbath as a time to put God first, honoring Him with the first fruits of your time for the week, seeking to do His will and doing good to others, then you can expect the blessing He promises: "you shall take delight in the Lord, and I will make you ride on the heights of the earth… for the mouth of the Lord has spoken" (Isaiah 58:14).

TAKE AWAY

- Don't work on the Sabbath if you have a choice.
- Do good on the Sabbath; care for the critical needs of others.
- Take time to worship and rest on the Sabbath, as you desperately need the benefits that come from doing these things to function in a healthy way as a Christian, as a human, and as a business owner. Worship and rest can provide the inspiration and energy you need to operate your business.

COMMANDMENT 5

# HONOR YOUR FATHER *and* MOTHER

*"Honor your father and your mother, that your days may be long in the land that the Lord your God is giving you." —Exodus 20:12*

There are two main points of application for your business that I find embedded in this commandment. First, consider the second part of this verse: "That your days may be long in the land that the Lord your God is giving you." God advises us to honor our parents, among many reasons, for the fact that parental wisdom and guidance can spare us a great deal of pain and suffering from harmful and foolish decisions.

As a child, your parents likely warned you against the hazards of taking candy from strangers. As a result, you probably made it a habit to steer clear of any unfamiliar adults who offered you a lollipop, a ride in their car, or anything else smacking of suspicion. Because your parents were aware of the realities of kidnapping and murder, they gave you wise instructions to help preserve your life. As an adult, you are not necessarily dependent upon your parents' advice to keep you alive, however, their life experience can continue to be an asset to you as you conduct your life and your business. Parental advice, at all stages of life, can be very valuable.

When I was a young child, my mother spent hours upon hours teaching me truths from the Bible and helping me to memorize Scriptures that have remained with me to this day. When I first started my business, I found myself becoming burned out, confused, and exhausted. In the end, I only found relief and healing when the biblical truths that my mother had instilled in me as a child, once again took center stage in my life, guiding both my business and everything else. Your parents may not be experts in your field of expertise, but that does not disqualify them from offering deeply beneficial counsel to you that may spare you stress and suffering in the long run. Proverbs 30:17 offers a rather sharp admonition to heed the counsel of one's parents, "The eye that mocks a father and scorns to obey a mother will be picked out by the ravens of the valley and eaten by the vultures." A graphic depiction it is indeed of those who reject the wisdom of their father and mother.

The second consideration regarding honoring one's parents is based upon Mark 7, in which Jesus rebukes the Pharisees for neglecting the care of their aging parents, giving the money that would have been spent to supply their daily necessities to the temple instead.

> *"And he [Jesus] said to them, 'Well did Isaiah prophesy of you hypocrites, as it is written, "'This people honors me with their lips, but their heart is far from me; in vain do they worship me, teaching as doctrines the commandments of men.' You leave the commandment of God and hold to the tradition of men." And he said to them, "You have a fine way of rejecting the commandment of God in order to establish your tradition! For Moses said, 'Honor your father and your*

> *mother'; and, 'Whoever reviles father or mother must surely die.' But you say, 'If a man tells his father or his mother, "Whatever you would have gained from me is…given to God…then you no longer permit him to do anything for his father or mother, thus making void the word of God by your tradition that you have handed down. And many such things you do"''* (Mark 7:6-13).

Among several principles Jesus is teaching in this passage, the fact that He expects us to care for the needs of our families, including our parents, is undeniably evident. Yet, how often do we set aside the responsibility of properly caring for our families in order to care instead for our businesses?

In addition to understanding the principles of honor and care as they relate to physical needs, it is important to note that the command to honor our parents has the implication of treating them with an air of dignity and respect. Under Mosaic law, the punishment for reviling or criticizing parents in an abusive or angrily insulting manner was death. From this, we realize that we must refrain from abusive critiques of our parents and instead, offer them positive comments, dignity, respect, and a measure of priority. Think for a moment how often, in the name of business, you will decline a call from a parent or family member, when you would quickly take a call from a customer or an employee? Or have you just been so busy with your business that you haven't taken the time to visit your parents in a while?

No matter how dedicated you are to your work, you are still expected by God to meet the needs of your family first, before those of anyone else. If you cannot be faithful to care for those entrusted to you—your parents, your spouse, your children—how can you expect God to fully bless your efforts directed elsewhere? Think of it this way: the souls of your family will live on forever, but your business—regardless of how great or successful—has a very limited lifespan in comparison with the eternal one awaiting every human being. Do not invest all of your time in feeding that which is temporal while starving that which is eternal.

TAKE AWAY

- Your parents' counsel may be helpful for you in your business.
- Treat your parents with dignity, respect and priority and don't let your business crowd them out.
- Investing in people, especially those close to you, has eternal value which is greater than business value.

COMMANDMENT 6

# YOU SHALL NOT MURDER

*"You shall not murder." —Exodus 20:13*

At first glance, this commandment would seem to be one that most of us could consider ourselves guiltless of transgressing. Upon inspection of it in the broader context of the whole of Scripture, it becomes apparent that each of us are indeed culpable regarding the keeping of this mandate. How can this be? In the Sermon on the Mount, Jesus offered us some very hard-hitting teaching regarding the Law and the Commandments, saying of the sixth commandment:

> *"You have heard that it was said to those of old, 'You shall not murder; and whoever murders will be liable to*

> *judgment.' But I say to you that everyone who is angry with his brother will be liable to judgment; whoever insults his brother will be liable to the council; and whoever says, 'You fool!' will be liable to the hell of fire" (Matthew 5:21-22).*

Additionally, 1 John 3:15 states, "Everyone who hates his brother is a murderer, and you know that no murderer has eternal life abiding in him." According to these two passages, it becomes apparent that God equates the sins of anger and hatred with that of murder. It may seem preposterous in our minds to judge these sins in this manner, but consider this: do not each of those sins spring from the same type of blackness found in the heart of unregenerate man? Is it not hatred—a lack of love for others—that causes us to harbor anger and resentment for our brother, or to take his life? God knows the human heart better than we ourselves do, and it is for this reason that He has revealed that both hatred and murder are the same transgression and are worthy of hell.

We may ask, what is hatred? As hatred is the opposite of love, perhaps a working definition of love would help us understand its dichotomous opposition. 1 Corinthians 13:4-8 says:

> *"Love is patient and kind; love does not envy or boast; it is not arrogant or rude. It does not insist on its own way; it is not irritable or resentful; it does not rejoice at wrongdoing, but rejoices with the truth. Love bears all things, believes all things, hopes all things, endures all things. Love never ends."*

If love is all of these things, then hatred must be impatient and unkind, envious and boastful, arrogant and rude. It insists on its own way, it is irritable and resentful. It rejoices with wrongdoing and delights in falsehood. It bears nothing, believes nothing, hopes nothing, and endures nothing. Does this description match any of your behavior toward others, perhaps toward specific others? If so, it would be wise to examine your heart to see if the plague of hatred has begun its ravaging work in your being. It can invade your dearest relationships and reduce them to heaps of smoldering ashes. If you find hatred abiding in your heart toward anyone—whether a spouse, an employee, a client, or any other person—you must act swiftly and decisively to ensure that its flames are sufficiently extinguished, before irreversible damage is done.

I know from personal and professional experience that almost every business has at least one customer that brings the business owner a large measure of grief. Do you have a customer that has frustrated you to the point of developing hatred? Maybe you have been betrayed by a trusted employee and the ruins of the relationship have left behind a festering wound of hate for him or her? Probably the deepest business hatred that I've seen is among ex-business partners. Just like the hatred that is often found in domestic divorces, business partnership divorces frequently have high emotional stakes and can end with hatred on both parties.

You simply cannot expect to experience God's best for your business if you are harboring hatred or bitterness toward anyone, including people that you know through your business. Matthew 5:23-24 tells us exactly what to do if we have a problem with hatred or bitterness: "So if you are offering your gift at the altar and there remember that your brother has something against you, leave your gift there before the altar and go. First be reconciled to your brother, and then come and offer your gift."

Often, the first step toward working through hatred involves forgiving someone of an egregious offense against you. Matthew 18:21-22 says, "Then Peter came up and said to him, 'Lord, how often will my brother sin against me, and I forgive him? As many as seven times?' Jesus said to him, 'I do not say to you seven times, but seventy-seven times.'" Doubtless, this is a hard pill to swallow, but the alternative to forgiveness is to engage in sin ourselves by living with unresolved hatred and bitterness, in violation of Scripture. May the Lord help us to forgive others, just as He has forgiven us. We could never have deserved the forgiveness that God has freely offered to us. In the same way, the person who is the object of your hatred may not deserve forgiveness either, and that's fine. As C.S. Lewis said so insightfully, "To be a Christian means to forgive the inexcusable, because God has forgiven the inexcusable in you" (p. 182, 1949). Forgive the offenses of others, regardless of whether or not they deserve it, and you can be free of hatred.

If we determine that we are indeed in bondage to the sin of hate, 1 John 1:9 encourages us with these words: "If we confess our sins, he is faithful and just to forgive us our sins and to cleanse us from all unrighteousness." There is no hatred too dark or too deep that God is unable to work healing and reconciliation in its place when we come before Him with a repentant heart.

TAKE AWAY

- Hatred is a sin as serious as murder.
- Forgive those who have wronged you in business or in other ways, just as God has forgiven you.
- Do not harbor hatred or bitterness toward anyone including customers, vendors, employees or partners.

COMMANDMENT 7

# You Shall Not Commit Adultery

*"You shall not commit adultery." —Exodus 20:14*

At first glance, the connection between the sin of adultery and your business might not seem to be significant—in fact, it may appear that there is no real connection between the two at all. However, there are actually several key ways in which the sin of adultery can spell ruin for your business, and even more consequentially, for your life.

First and most importantly, if you engage in the sin of adultery, you corrupt yourself and your relationship with Christ. 1 Corinthians 6:18-20 says this:

> *"Flee from sexual immorality. Every other sin a person commits is outside the body, but the sexually immoral person sins against his own body. Or do you not know that your body is a temple of the Holy Spirit within you, whom you have from God? You are not your own, for you were bought with a price. So glorify God in your body."*

As a Christian, you are to uphold the highest standard of moral character in keeping with the will of God, as revealed in the commands of Scripture. 2 Peter 2:19 says, "For whatever overcomes a person, to that he is enslaved." Obviously, if you are being ruled by the Holy Spirit, you will not be following the lusts of the flesh, leading to sexual immorality. Conversely, if you find yourself being overcome by passions *not* consistent with the desires of God, you can easily determine that you are being enslaved to the powers of darkness. This reason alone should be more than sufficient motivation to keep your heart diligently focused on preserving your moral and sexual purity. However, the Scriptures are not finished yet with expounding the repercussions of marital infidelity.

The sin of adultery, when discovered, is almost certain to demolish your credibility and your witness as a Christian.

While you may be fully repentant of your immorality, in the eyes of those who trusted and admired you as a fellow believer in Christ, you will lose all clout. God may forgive you, but the consequences of your sin will dog your steps and may spell destruction for your business. Proverbs 6:27-28 offers this warning to those who engage in adultery, naively thinking that what they do will not hurt them or others: "Can a man carry fire next to his chest and his clothes not be burned? Or can one walk on hot coals and his feet not be scorched?" A few verses later, the passage continues, "He who commits adultery lacks sense; he who does it destroys himself. *He will get wounds and dishonor, and his disgrace will not be wiped away*." (Proverbs 6:32-33, italics added). Hitting a bit closer to home, you may suffer loss to your business as clients choose to take their work elsewhere, judging that your lack of integrity in one area of your life may indicate immorality in other aspects of your life and work, of which they want no part.

Unfortunately, I personally know of several business owners who have lost their businesses as a result of adultery. What the Scriptures say is true. You cannot expect to engage in the sin of adultery without any negative consequences for your life or your business. As we just saw, the Word tells us that the adulterer "destroys himself" (Proverbs 6:32). For a business owner, that destruction usually includes the downfall of your business as well.

If you have committed adultery in the past, but have subsequently expressed genuine repentance and sought with every bit of your being to make amends to everyone who has been hurt as a result of your immorality, and have found reconciliation and forgiveness both with God and with those affected by your sin, then God be praised! As Jesus instructed the woman caught in adultery in John 8:11, "Go, and from now on sin no more." However, if you find yourself reading this discourse on the evils of adultery and are tempted to delude yourself that none of it applies to you since you have remained faithful to your spouse or since you are not married at all, I exhort you to consider the heart-root of adultery and then examine yourself to determine whether or not you are guilty of the same attitude of the heart that engenders adultery. That attitude is one of self-indulgence, greed, and lack of restraint and self-control; it can be manifested in the sins of lust, addictions, gluttony, fornication, and monetary greed, among others. Any of these sins can be as destructive to one's life and business as that of adultery. A heart ruled by intemperance and unsanctified passions can be capable of all types of evil.

There is a practical point of caution for business owners stemming from this commandment. As we know, sin has its inception in the mind and heart, not in the body (James 1:14-15). We see evidence of this principle again in Matthew 15:19: "For out of the heart come evil thoughts, murder, adultery, sexual immorality, theft, false witness, slander." Understanding that sin starts with the mind and heart and that entertaining evil thoughts precedes the execution of evil actions, we need to take every thought captive to the obedience of Christ (2 Corinthians 10:5). If you are able to quell carnality at the thought level, then it will never have the opportunity to manifest itself on the physical level. Do not allow lustful or impure thoughts to linger, but instead flee from them (1 Corinthians 6:18).

Thankfully, as utterly destructive as adultery can be, there are practical steps that can be taken and safeguards that can be put into practice that can protect you from being overcome with passion in a moment of weakness and, as a result, doing something that tarnishes your reputation, your life, and the name of Christ. Current (as of the time of this writing) Vice President of the United States, Mike Pence, was quoted in March 2017, as having a personal policy that he will not eat dinner alone with a woman who is not his wife (*The Washington Post*, 2017). While he endured extensive abuse from the media for this practice, his commitment to honoring his wife and his marriage through this practice is remarkable. Especially as someone in a position of power and visibility, Pence could easily be the target of malicious rumor. However, by keeping this policy, he both safeguards himself from sin, and slams shut the door to speculation and slander.

As a business owner in a position of prominence and visibility, you should realize that there might be those who would seek to make you the target of slander. It would be wise to heed the example of VP Pence in shutting the door to rumors by leading a life of transparency and accountability. Evangelist Billy Graham had a similar policy—he refused even to ride in an elevator alone with a woman. In the same way, take the necessary practical steps to protect yourself in moments of weakness from becoming an adulterer, whose ruin is described in Proverbs 7:22-23:

> *"As an ox goes to the slaughter, or as a stag is caught fast till an arrow pierces its liver; as a bird rushes into a snare; he does not know that it will cost him his life."*

One policy I have adopted over the years is to refrain from touching women other than my wife or immediate family members. The only exceptions are a handshake, or what is generally termed a "Christian side hug"—and then only if initiated by the other person.

Additionally, in today's interconnected culture, inappropriate emotional relationships can begin within the relative privacy of texting, social media messaging, and email. Emotional intimacy with members of the opposite sex outside of marriage is adultery in the making. Avoid private emotional conversations with members of the opposite gender, whether in person or via some technological medium. Do not give place to seemingly innocent private conversations, lest those relationships slide down a slippery slope, becoming an emotional bond that is followed by an adulterous physical connection. To facilitate transparency and accountability in my life, my cell phone and laptop are considered public property in my home. Everyone in the house knows my passwords and at any time, my wife and children have access to and may use my devices. The presence of safeguards has been a powerful aid in protecting the treasure of unbroken fidelity in my marriage.

Spend some time deciding what safeguards you need to implement to keep yourself free from adultery. For you, it may mean refusing to spend time working alone with certain co-workers. It may mean always bringing one of your children or family members along with you on business trips. It may mean instituting a no-touching policy, or perhaps having your cell company send copies of all of your texts to your spouse. Whatever it takes, keep yourself pure and blameless and flee from intimacy with anyone other than your spouse, whether emotional or physical.

Before leaving this discussion, it seems appropriate to deal with one of the most under-addressed challenges and addictions raging in our society. While interacting with pornography is sometimes dismissed by users as being morally justifiable because the viewer is not actually engaging in a physical act, if we adhere to the stance that Jesus made clear in the Sermon on the Mount, we must realize that it is indeed a morally reprehensible activity. Matthew 5:38 reads:

> *"But I say to you that everyone who looks at a woman with a lustful intent has already committed adultery with her in his heart."*

Clearly, pornography causes its viewers to think thoughts that fit squarely within this description, and therefore, porn usage itself is considered adultery according to this standard. Taking it a step further, pornography use has been correlated with an increase in marital infidelity of more than 300%. According to another statistic, 56% of divorces involve one party having an obsessive interest in porn (2010). Lest we attribute the bulk of porn consumption to the unchurched, statistics from a study commissioned by Josh McDowell Ministries and Covenant Eyes demonstrate that 64% of youth pastors and 57% of pastors have struggled with pornography either currently or in the past (DeHaas, 2016). A great way to guard against the destructive force of pornography is to implement an accountability reporting software tool like Accountable2You or Covenant Eyes. Both of these tools were created by believers to support other Christians in their efforts to stand firm against temptation and stay pure before the Lord and their spouses. Setting safeguards like these to avoid pornography can help couples remain faithful to one another and maintain a clear conscience before God.

Failing to keep this commandment regarding adultery can destroy your marriage, your reputation, your Christian witness, your relationship with your children, and of course, your business, so take the greatest care to guard your business and your heart against any lustful or adulterous thoughts or actions.

TAKE AWAY

- Adultery will destroy both you and your business.
- Sin begins in the mind and heart, and lust is akin to adultery.
- Christian business owners (and Christians in general) need physical barriers and communication safeguards to help avoid adultery.

COMMANDMENT 8

# You Shall Not Steal

*"You shall not steal." —Exodus 20:15*

Unless you grew up in a poverty-stricken family in which you were taught to steal in order to survive, or unless your parents were unremorseful mobsters who stole from, lied to, and extorted people on a day-to-day basis, you were probably raised with the general ideal that stealing is wrong. As a result, you have probably never been to prison for such crimes as embezzlement, robbery, or the like. If you are like most people, having such a background does not mean that you have never stolen anything—perhaps a piece of candy from the drug store counter or a toy from a friend's house. But those incidents happened in your childhood or adolescence, and you've left those ways behind...right?

Sometimes, we allow our consciences to grow callous to forms of stealing that are not as blatant, or as seemingly consequential as the most obvious ones—we tend to think that since we are not Bernie Madoff or Al Capone, we are relatively innocent of stealing. While I do not wish to ignore the seriousness of the most outright forms of stealing, such as robbery, extortion, and embezzlement, neither do I want to focus on them to the exclusion of other forms of stealing that, while less heinous, are far more likely to be blots upon our own records.

Before we address specific ways in which stealing can take place, it is vital to offer a working definition of what it means to steal. Stealing goes far beyond the actual act of apprehending something that belongs to someone else. A helpful definition coined by Robert Deffinbaugh reads thus: "Stealing is getting ahead at another person's expense" or, more conceptually, "[t]aking from others without giving in return" (2004).

With this definition proposed, it is appropriate to speak to the most dangerous of these "lesser" forms of stealing first—that of stealing from God. Paying tithes—giving to the church in order to pay the pastors who minster to us and in order to further the work of the Lord—has always been an important principle by which God's people are expected to abide (Genesis 14:20; Malachi 3:10; Luke 20:25). Yet, when we skimp on giving God the full share that He is due, when we neglect to support the ministers who serve us through their work, we are doing a terrible thing—stealing from God and from His workers. If the Lord has blessed your business with profit, then He expects that you will render tithes to Him of those first fruits, as a way of honoring Him and recognizing that "every good and every perfect gift is from above" (James 1:17). Contrary to the message propagated by prosperity theology, we do not give to God in order to receive more from Him; instead we should give out of obedience and thankfulness to God. To avoid returning a portion to the Lord is to steal from Him, as Malachi 3:8 makes clear: "Will man rob God? Yet you are robbing me. But you say, 'How have we robbed you?' In your tithes and contributions."

Clearly, withholding one's money from God is a form of stealing, but did you know that withholding praise from God is also a serious form of stealing, one which is punishable by death. Acts 12:20-23 relates the following story:

> *"Now Herod was angry with the people of Tyre and Sidon, and they came to him with one accord, and having persuaded Blastus, the king's chamberlain, they asked for peace, because their country depended on the king's country for food. On an appointed day Herod put on his royal robes, took his seat upon the throne, and delivered an oration to them. And the people were shouting, "The voice of a god, and not of a man!" Immediately an angel of the Lord struck him down, because he did not give God the glory, and he was eaten by worms and breathed his last."*

How many times have you begged God for His help in a situation, and, by His grace, things ended up favorably for you? In the moments following, when those around you, witnessing your success, congratulated you on a job well done, did you simply bask in the glow of the moment, absorbing the praise, without deflecting any to the God who enabled your success, or did you instead give the credit for the achievement where it was due? To neglect to do so would be a form of stealing, would it not? Such sin is, in fact, considered so serious, that God punished King Herod with death as a result of his committing it.

Further, a common form of stealing can manifest itself at our places of work, with both time theft and petty theft. Estimating generously on timecards or using business property for personal purposes is wrong, even when it seems justifiable—"They don't pay me enough anyway," or "It's such a small theft, no one would ever notice."

One specific way in which small business owners should be particularly careful to keep their dealings honest with others concerns the way in which they compensate their employees. Consider what James 5:1-6 has to say about this matter:

> *"Come now, you rich, weep and howl for the miseries that are coming upon you. Your riches have rotted and your garments are moth-eaten. Your gold and silver have corroded, and their corrosion will be evidence against you and will eat your flesh like fire. You have laid up treasure in the last days. Behold, the wages of the laborers who mowed your fields, which you kept back by fraud, are crying out against you, and the cries of the harvesters have reached the ears of the Lord of hosts. You have lived on the earth in luxury and in self-indulgence. You have fattened your hearts in a day of slaughter. You*

> *have condemned and murdered the righteous person. He does not resist you."*

It is glaringly obvious from this passage, that to withhold fair wages from an employee is an inexcusable and serious offense that is sure to incur God's judgment. As an employer, you must take special care to appropriately pay those who work for you, knowing that you will be answerable to God for that which you have failed to rightfully render to them. I once knew an employer who wrote so many bad checks to his employees that at some point, they refused to accept checks from him any longer, demanding to be paid only in cash. As employers, we have an obligation not only to our team, but to God Himself to pay our employees fairly, and at the promised times.

Additionally, stealing from the government in the form of cheating on one's taxes is sinful and has no place in the life of a Christian. Often, business owners will justify their choice to cheat on their taxes by pleading that they are heavily and unfairly taxed, and that to do so is a way of restoring justice, in a sense. They may also complain that the government wastes a vast amount of the money that they amass in taxes, and some even see cheating on their taxes as a way of "punishing" the government. To that end, however, it must be made abundantly clear that layering wrongdoing on top of wrongdoing never makes a righteous action. Even if our own government practices poor stewardship, we are still under obligation to God to "render to Caesar the things that are Caesar's" (Mark 12:17). In his book, *Debt Free Living*, Larry Burkett shares a story about a car dealer who had been cheating on his taxes for many years and as a result, owed a tremendous sum to the government. After the Lord convicted this man of his sin, he repented before God and the government and made arrangements for the IRS to apprehend his business and all of his property. Once his assets had been seized, however, it was discovered that the land upon which the car dealership had stood held oil reserves, which allowed the man's IRS debt to be settled almost immediately! The Lord blessed the car dealer's obedience by providing for his debt to be satisfied with a "ram in the thicket" that he previously didn't know existed. While it was terribly difficult for this man to confess his sin and make amends, knowing that to do so would ruin him financially, he chose to be obedient to God no matter the cost, and

God honored him by providing a way for the debt to be ameliorated. If you know that you have been cheating the government, do not be afraid to confess your sin and make restitution—God will honor you if you make obedience to Him your top priority!

Now that we understand the different forms that stealing can take, it will be beneficial for us to explore *why* stealing is such a serious offense against God. In order to understand the biggest reason why this is the case, consider the following passage:

> *"Now as they were eating, Jesus took bread, and after blessing it broke it and gave it to the disciples, and said, "Take, eat; this is my body." And he took a cup, and when he had given thanks he gave it to them, saying, "Drink of it, all of you, for this is my blood of the covenant, which is poured out for many for the forgiveness of sins" (Matthew 26:28-26).*

Take a moment to ponder on the character of Jesus as demonstrated here. In this night, as throughout His entire life, He poured Himself out completely to others, giving everything that was His—even His own body and blood—so that we could benefit from a sacrifice which we could never in a million years deserve. If we are to call ourselves Christians, striving to walk in the ways of our Master, how can we consider the way in which Jesus completely *gave* of Himself, and then turn around and *take* from others, hurting them in order to gain something for ourselves? Would not such behavior be utterly nauseating to the God who, with immeasurable selflessness, love, and kindness, freely and gladly gave up everything so that we, pitiful and wretched creatures, could benefit from His suffering? The act of taking from others and therefore causing them to suffer runs completely contrary to the nature of God, who always gives sacrificially. Perhaps it is this truth, more than any other that explains why God looks upon stealing so severely.

Additionally, stealing is a crime that not only hurts the one being preyed upon, it also destroys the thief, as he incurs the wrath of God, as well as the wrath of other people for his unjust acts. While the thief plans to prosper from his wrongdoing, he always pays the price for sin, whether in this life or in the next, unless he repents of and amends his ways, finding forgiveness through Christ's blood.

Further, the act of stealing belies a lack of faith in God as our Provider. Often, we grow impatient in waiting for God to move, to meet our needs, to provide those things we long for more than anything else. When we begin to doubt His ability to provide, or His wisdom in knowing the proper time in which to supply what we need, we stoop to unsavory methods to procure that which we should wait upon God to provide or that for which God desires us to work to attain.

If you know that you have stolen, regardless of size or consequence, seek to follow the biblical rectification for stealing and make proper restitution to those harmed by your thievery. No doubt, to do this will be a humbling experience, but in the eyes of God, that is a very good thing, as it is written, "God opposes the proud, but gives grace to the humble" (James 4:6 and 1 Peter 5:5). As you probably learned from your childhood, there is no worse feeling than unresolved guilt and no better feeling than pure relief from carrying that burden. Hearkening back to the story shared earlier in this chapter, once the car dealer had confessed his crimes and made restitution, he proclaimed the goodness of being free of his burden of guilt. He craved that relief to such an extent that he was willing to give up all his worldly possessions in order to gain a clean conscience before the Lord. Breaking the power of sin through confession and repentance brings unparalleled peace and consolation.

Ephesians 4:28 instructs us:

> *"Let the thief no longer steal, but rather let him labor, doing honest work with his own hands, so that he may have something to share with anyone in need."*

Rather than seeking benefit for yourself by taking from others, instead work diligently so that you may, out of love and care for others, be an instrument of God to provide for their needs with generosity. After all, if we are to follow in Christ's steps, we should seek to be *givers*, as He is, rather than *takers*, as it is our sinful nature to be.

As business owners, there are a couple of specific considerations that we should mention here. First, it is important to realize that being in the position of a business owner can create a host of opportunities for what may be termed "shadowy theft." Shadowy theft can be defined as taking something in such way that it is considered legally permissible, though probably not ethically permissible. As believers, we answer first and foremost to God, a power that is higher than the law of the land. Just because human law may allow me to do something that is morally objectionable does not mean it is an action pleasing to God and therefore something I *should* do. My grandfather used to say that if you have to really split hairs to determine whether something is or is not a sin, chances are, it probably *is* a sin. Business owners have the legal ability to rationally over-charge a customer, to not issue a refund after an accidental overpayment, to short a shipment, or to do any number of possible things. While these actions don't seem to be on the same level of severity as breaking in to someone's building and stealing property, they still qualify in the eyes of God as stealing. In business, abide by the Golden Rule in treating others as you want to be treated, meaning in large part, that you refuse to deal with others in any way other than with total honesty.

The second and last point for business owners is to realize that although *you* may deal fairly with others and would never steal from anyone, there *are* those who give off the appearance of honesty that do desire to steal from you. With decades of public accounting experience, I have seen many cases of embezzlement. In the most recent case, the embezzler was a highly trusted family friend and an employee with many years of honest service. Amazingly, this thief stole over $250,000 from her friends and employer over the course of three years. Don't think that professing Christians are not immune to stealing. Over the years, I've seen many congregations fall victim to having funds stolen by a church financial secretary. I have also seen two separate cases where pastor's wives have embezzled from their employers. Do not blindly trust that others will abide by a scrupulous standard of integrity simply because they attend church and seem to be decent, Christian people. Instead, construct safeguards and internal control mechanisms to help minimize the opportunity for others to steal from you. Remember: stealing goes against the very nature of God, who is a giver. Do not steal in any form or fashion.

TAKE AWAY

- Do not steal from God; return to Him what He is due.
- Do not steal from employees (or vendors, customers, banks, etc.).
- Avoid shadowy theft. Avoid legal thievery and hold to God's standard, not man's standard. If you think a certain manner of dealing might be wrong and be some sort of theft, then cease those dealings.
- Protect your business from embezzlement and other forms of theft.

COMMANDMENT 9

# You Shall Not Lie

*"You shall not bear false witness against your neighbor."*
*—Exodus 20:16*

There are some things that just seem obviously wrong, like killing another human being in cold blood, or stealing an elderly person's life savings. When we hear of those crimes being committed, a sense of justice within us is stirred up and we feel, deep in our hearts, that to do such a thing is to be worthy of a hefty punishment. The act of lying, however, is often one that we can engage in without much crisis of conscience, especially when the lie is small and seemingly inconsequential. If you told your spouse that you had already paid a bill in order to keep them off your back, even if you had not done it yet, but had every intention of getting to it tomorrow, would you stay awake that night with a nagging feeling of guilt that would compel you to rectify your untruth? Most of us would like to believe that we speak truthfully and that what we say can always be trusted. We also realize that we're only human, and that slips-of-the-tongue or white lies can escape our lips almost more quickly than we can think them. When this happens, it is easy to excuse these mistakes as the failings of an otherwise moral person, rather than as the rotten fruit of a heart inclined to do evil.

If we take the Bible at face value, then we should fully understand that lying, in any form or fashion, is wrong under any circumstances. Period. End of story. However, we seem to so easily find justification for our deceptions—and for what appear to be good reasons. We think about instances in which good, godly people were compelled to lie under dire circumstances in order to save the lives of others and wonder how their actions could be considered sinful, since by them, others benefited. At first, God's command to "love your neighbor" (Matthew 22:39) seems sometimes to run in contradiction to His prohibitions against telling lies. To this end, Sarah Sumner offers an insightful perspective, "What... [the fact that heroic Christians told lies to accomplish great things] shows is not that lying is honoring to God, but rather that human circumstances can degenerate into something so depraved that lies get mixed in with acts of faith" (2011). God used them despite their failings, not because of them.

In business especially, there is often a tendency to let the policy of absolute honesty slide a bit. Perhaps the advertisement needn't be completely truthful—after all, the benefits of the product outweigh the drawbacks, right? Potential investors needn't know all of the possible negative outcomes that could result if the venture goes poorly. There are so many excuses that can be made for smudging the truth. What we must come to understand and accept is that if we resolve to always tell the truth, things may sometimes be harder for us. It takes courage to speak the truth because it is not always what others want to hear, and it may not always give us what we want.

From God's perspective, of course, truth telling always leads to blessing, as obedience to God's commands pleases Him and invites His provision and mercy to be showered upon us. However, we should not be surprised if, at times, being honest in business is costly. Maybe the imperfections of a property we are trying to sell or owning up to a mistake causes us to lose a business deal or an important customer. Though this may be the case, when we are brave enough to be forthcoming with the truth, we should be encouraged that the Lord consistently honors those who honor Him.

In Corrie ten Boom's outstanding autobiography, *The Hiding Place*, she relates several stories in which God honored what would seem to be reckless honesty. She relates one particular story concerning her sister, Nollie, and her children. While Corrie chose to lie in order to protect herself and the Jews that she was hiding, Nollie held to an unyielding standard of absolute honesty and taught her children to abide by the same standard. Once, when German soldiers came to commandeer Nollie's sons to join Hitler's army, the boys quickly jumped down a trap door hidden under the kitchen table, covered with a rug, and appeared to be safe from detection. When one of the soldiers directly asked Nollie's daughter, "Where are your brothers?" she replied, "Why, they're under the table" (1971, pp. 90-91). Pulling back the tablecloth and seeing no one crouching underneath, the soldiers assumed that the girl was mocking them and left angrily, leaving the brothers undiscovered. When Nollie, who was absent during the event, heard what had happened, she exclaimed, "God honors truth-telling with perfect protection!" (1971, p. 91). As the story demonstrates, we can trust God to look after us, even in the most hopeless situations, if we will keep obedience to His commands our first priority.

But why, we may ask, is lying so wrong? Similar to stealing, lying is a terrible evil for the reason that it runs counter to God's own nature. 1 John 1:5 says poetically, "God is light, and in Him is no darkness at all" and Hebrews 6:18 tells us bluntly, "It is impossible for God to lie." Conversely, Jesus says in John 8, speaking to the Pharisees, "You are of your father the devil, and your will is to do your father's desires. He was a murderer from the beginning, and does not stand in the truth, because there is no truth in him. When he lies, he speaks out of his own character, for he is a liar and the father of lies" (verse 44). It follows then, that when we tell lies, we are becoming partakers in the nature and the realm of the devil, from whose grasp we have been saved. As 2 Peter 2:22 says very appropriately, "What the true proverb says has happened to them [those who return to sin after claiming the name of Christ]: 'The dog returns to its own vomit, and the sow, after washing herself, returns to wallow in the mire.'" Instead, we are called to be "partakers of the *divine nature*, having escaped from the corruption that is in the world because of sinful desire" (2 Peter 1:4, italics added). To tell lies is to isolate ourselves from fellowship with Christ and from participating in His nature—no lie is worth that!

Throughout my years in business, I've known clients who are professing believers to actually boast about the lies they have told as part of their business dealings. They believe that their deception makes them shrewd business people; unfortunately, all it makes them are liars; sinners in need of repentance, forgiveness and a turning away from falsehood.

One particularly common lie in business can be seen when a person is trying to avoid speaking with someone; often whoever is taking the call is instructed to report that the person wanted on the telephone is "out," even when they are clearly "in." Would it not be better to simply state that a person is "unavailable" or "is not taking calls at the moment?" There is no need to lie. Tolerance and propagation of small lies within a company can quickly lead to dishonesty on a greater scale. Further, asking your employees to lie for you in this manner will cause them to lose respect for you and will breed a company culture of dishonesty. After watching you smear the truth when convenient, your employees will start to question why they should not lie to you about being "out sick." In business, such a culture of deceit is destructive on many levels. It is always best to be honest; doing so will invite the Lord's blessing rather than His judgment.

You may, at this point, be feeling convicted by "little" lies that you have told, ones that perhaps you excused as being insignificant, both in the eyes of God and man. If this is the case, then simply follow the instructions found in Ephesians 4:25, "Therefore, having put away falsehood, let each one of you speak the truth with his neighbor, for we are members one of another." Confess your untruths, speak truth, and seek forgiveness and you will find healing and blessing.

Before this discussion is ended, please allow room for an important caveat to be named. Specifically, make it your mission to follow the instructions of Colossians 4:6: "Let your speech always be *gracious*, seasoned with salt, so that you may know how you ought to answer each person" (italics added). Rather than simply speaking every thought—good or bad, kind or rude—that occurs to your mind in the name of honesty, instead, consider the effect that your words will have on others. Will your words direct them toward the goodness of God and glorification of Christ, or will they cause strife and division, both of which are unfitting for God's holy people (Ephesians 4:1-3). While the preservation of unity is no excuse for telling lies, honesty is no excuse for unloving or unkind speech. "Rather, speaking the truth in love, we are to grow up in every way into Him who is the head, into Christ" (Ephesians 4:15). Let both the truth and the grace of God guide your speech!

TAKE AWAY

- Lies of any size or consequence are not to be tolerated and will not ultimately be profitable.
- Always deal honestly with customers, employees and vendors. Dishonesty will eventually be uncovered and can destroy your business and witness.
- A culture of dishonesty is created when the business owner tells blatant lies, as well as when he or she asks others to lie for them, regardless of how small the lies might seem.
- Just because something is true, does not mean it merits utterance.

COMMANDMENT 10

# YOU SHALL NOT COVET

*"You shall not covet your neighbor's house; you shall not covet your neighbor's wife, or his male servant, or his female servant, or his ox, or his donkey, or anything that is your neighbor's." —Exodus 20:17*

Of the Ten Commandments, this one may be the most directly opposed to the contemporary perspective of the American dream. In a society where materialistic desires and cutthroat strategies intended to obtain the objects of one's all-consuming lust for money, power, and prestige are applauded and rewarded, it's no surprise that the biblical view of worldly goods is exceedingly unpopular. If you have ever seen the television show, "Shark Tank," then you have observed a prime example of individuals who have attained the pinnacle of the American ideal—being fabulously wealthy and enormously influential, and yet some of the sharks lack graciousness in a glaring capacity. Many people aspire to be like the sharks, having great wealth, possessions, and power. But, we may ask, what value are those things if they erode your Christian character?

While it is certainly not sinful to work diligently to provide for oneself and one's family, nor is it wrong to become wealthy as a result of that work, it *is* however, unfitting for Christians to be consumed by a desire for that which others have, letting that lust corrode their lives and entice them to sin even further. Every sin begins with a spark, which can either be stamped out immediately or fanned into a blazing furnace. As it is written in James 1:14-15, "But each person is tempted when he is lured and enticed by his own desire. Then desire when it has conceived gives birth to sin, and sin when it is fully grown brings forth death." Our key responsibility is to guard our hearts so that seeds of discontentment are rooted out and that righteous desires are cultivated and brought to fruition.

As you might expect, the Scriptures have a great deal to say on the topic of covetousness. Colossians 3:5 says plainly, "Put to death therefore what is earthly in you: sexual immorality, impurity, passion, evil desire, and covetousness, which is idolatry." It should be no surprise to us that covetousness is described here as a form of idolatry. The presence of any overwhelming desire—other than a longing for God—indicates that something besides the Lord has taken first place in our hearts and has become our master, ruling over us (2 Peter 2:19; Matthew 6:24).

In addition, covetousness—dissatisfaction with what God has given to you—is a form of rebellion that also belies a distrust in God's willingness and ability to provide for your needs. Psalm 78 recounts in full detail the actions of the Israelites described in Exodus 16 and Numbers 11. Here, the Israelites, having been graciously sustained by God in the wilderness through the daily provision of manna, begin to covet the delicacies that they once enjoyed in Egypt. They began to complain so severely that Moses implored God saying: "I am not able to carry all this people alone; the burden is too heavy for me. If you will treat me like this, kill me at once, if I find favor in your sight" (Numbers 11:14-15). Referring to this situation, Psalm 78:17-22 says:

> *"Yet they sinned still more against him,* rebelling *against the Most High in the desert. They tested God in their heart by demanding the food they craved. They spoke against God, saying, 'Can God spread a table in the wilderness? He struck the rock so that water gushed out and streams overflowed. Can he also give bread or provide meat for his people?' Therefore, when the Lord heard, he was full of wrath; a fire was kindled against Jacob; his anger rose against Israel,* ***because they did not believe in God and did not trust his saving power"*** *(emphasis added).*

It is true that there may be times in which you experience unfavorable circumstances, out of which you simply cannot seem to see a way of escape. In those times, understand that it is not wrong to petition God—even relentlessly so—to change your circumstances or to provide for your needs. In fact, to do so is commended throughout Scripture, as Luke 18:1-8 and Philippians 4:6-7 clearly demonstrate. It is never wrong to respectfully, yet boldly, make your requests known before the throne of God. After all, Jesus gave His life so that we could have confident access to our Father in heaven, as Ephesians 3:11-12 states:

> *"This was according to the eternal purpose that he has realized in Christ Jesus our Lord, in whom we have boldness and access with confidence through our faith in him."*

Hebrews 10:19-22 also says:

> *"Therefore, brothers, since we have confidence to enter the holy places by the blood of Jesus, by the new and living way that he opened for us through the curtain, that is, through his flesh, and since we have a great priest over the house of God, let us draw near with a true heart in full assurance of faith."*

The problem comes when we grumble with unthankful and faithless hearts, as the Israelites did, that God cannot or will not take care of His children, and when we cultivate cravings that run contrary to God's will for us. James 4 addresses this issue specifically, saying:

> *"What causes quarrels and what causes fights among you? Is it not this, that your passions are at war within*

> *you? You desire and do not have, so you murder. You covet and cannot obtain, so you fight and quarrel. You do not have, because you do not ask. You ask and do not receive, because you ask wrongly, to spend it on your passions."*

From this, we can understand that it is not the *asking* that displeases God, but the carnal passions—specifically covetousness—that reside in our hearts that cause us to sin. It does say, "You do not have, because you do not ask" (James 4:2). This indicates that we are to ask for what we need, but the rest of the passage indicates that those things we *desire* from God should be things consistent with a sanctified heart and sanctified passions. This means that asking God to give you a million dollars so that you can buy a Lamborghini would probably be wrong, coming from a heart ruled by covetousness, while asking Him to give you favor with your clients so that you can better serve them and provide for your family, would likely be much more in line with the will of God, and therefore, more likely to be granted.

By nature, most business owners are ambitious people. So, how can Christian business owners balance their sense of healthy ambition with a spirit of contentment so as to avoid becoming covetous? How can we simultaneously desire God's best for our business and still be content with our current state? To have ambition without coveting requires a certain level of spiritual maturity that allows a person to delineate between the acquisition of material goods and a sense of success. Success as a Christian business owner can be understood as reaching your maximum God-given potential in fulfilling God's chosen purpose for you. The Lord may desire you to have a company that employs 2 people, 20 people, 200 or 2,000. The number of employees you retain and size the of your business are not important. What *is* important is being obedient and faithful to God in all that He has called you to do, without coveting the material possessions of others. God has entrusted your business to you for the purpose of providing for yourself and others, and for that of making disciples. It does not exist to elevate your personal socioeconomic status; material wealth may be a by-product of our faithfulness, given by the graciousness and blessing of God, but it should never be the ultimate goal. Rather, our goal as Christian business owners should be to spread the Gospel and to make more disciples.

As the Apostle Paul wrote:

> *"I have learned in whatever situation I am to be content. I know how to be brought low, and I know how to abound. In any and every circumstance, I have learned the secret of facing plenty and hunger, abundance and need. I can do all things through him who strengthens me...And my God will supply every need of yours according to his riches in glory in Christ Jesus" (Philippians 4:11-13, 19).*

When we have Christ, we are supplied with more than enough to sustain us, both in this life and in the next. 1 Timothy 6:6-10 offers this wisdom:

> *"But godliness with contentment is great gain, for we brought nothing into the world, and we cannot take anything out of the world. But if we have food and clothing, with these we will be content. But those who desire to be rich fall into temptation, into a snare, into many senseless and harmful desires that plunge people into ruin and destruction. For the love of money is a root of all kinds of evils. It is through this craving that some have wandered away from the faith and pierced themselves with many pangs."*

While we should live lives driven by a desire to advance the kingdom of God and to glorify Him, our desire for worldly riches should be tempered by our necessities—that we should not greedily desire more than is necessary for us to do the will of God.

Covetousness is not only destructive in that the desires themselves can corrode us (Proverbs 14:30)—but it can also wreck our lives by causing us to commit more sins as a consequence of those desires.

Throughout my many years of experience in business, I have known of several business people who have committed loan fraud, not motivated by financial desperation, but rather to fund the "American Dream," to help the business people to get ahead of their neighbor, so to speak.

I've seen some clients go from making $50,000 per year and always being able to pay my invoice to making $200,000 per year and writing me bad checks. Why? Had their situations become desperate? Hardly. Instead, their covetous attitudes compelled them to consume more cars, clothes, and vacations than they could actually afford. Ecclesiastes 5:10 says, "He who loves money will not be satisfied with money, nor he who loves wealth with his income; this also is vanity." Plainly stated, when a covetous attitude is present, it does not matter how much income may be generated—the person will always spend beyond what they can afford! Sadly, coveting often leads to a lifestyle of overconsumption, which inevitably engenders major issues with debt and cash flow.

In contrast, one friend of mine, a fellow business owner, suddenly went from making $50,000 per year to almost $250,000 per year, yet he never altered his lifestyle to reflect his increased income, and as a result, he managed to save over $1,000,000 in just a few years! After a while, the company lost a key contract and the business was almost shuttered, yet, for this man, there was no cause for panic. After all, at his sustained rate of spending, his $1 million in savings should last him about 20 years, affording him plenty of time to restructure his business and find a new revenue stream. Had this man been a covetous business owner, he would likely have squandered the extra income on personal possessions instead of saving up for the future, and would probably not have fared as well when his business experienced a downturn.

Recorded in Joshua 7 is the story of a man named Achan who coveted the riches of the people inhabiting the land God had promised to the Israelites. As a result, when Joshua led the children of Israel into that land to conquer it, Achan took the opportunity to line his own pockets with the gold, silver, and fine clothes of those that they subdued, against God's commands. As one might expect, Achan's sin was exposed and God ordained that he and his whole household be stoned for the sin he had committed—a sad ending for a man whose actions seem understandably human to us. His weakness, we painfully realize, could well be our own. Micah 2:2 describes the depths of depravity to which we can easily be led, when blinded by covetousness: "They covet fields and seize them, and houses, and take them away; they oppress a man and his house, a man and his inheritance." Covetous desires can compel us to steal, to kill, or to commit any number of other equally appalling deeds. The greedy person will stop at nothing to satisfy his or her unquenchable desires, mowing down those who stand in his or her way.

As we seek to abandon covetous desires, we should also cultivate a heart of deep contentment with the provision that God has made for us. Rather than obsessing over how to get our hands on the newest sports car available, we ought instead to be thankful for the dependable Ford or Chevrolet that performs well for us on a daily basis. Rather than coveting a 10,000 square foot mansion, we should give thanks for the 1,200 square foot house that has been owned—debt-free—for the past several years, allowing financial freedom to give even more generously to God's work. Hebrews 13:5 says, "Keep your life free from love of money, and be content with what you have, for he has said, 'I will never leave you nor forsake you.' With Christ always encompassing us wherever we go, we are sure to have enough to sustain us, both spiritually and physically.

God knows what we most need. He understands what it is that satisfies us deeply and truly. We have a longing for that which only God can supply, but, in our stubborn thick-headedness, we never cease to try to satisfy this longing on our own with material items, with relationships—both good and bad—and even with addictions. In *The Weight of Glory*, C.S. Lewis writes:

> *"We are half-hearted creatures, fooling about with drink and sex and ambition when infinite joy is offered us, like*

> *an ignorant child who wants to go on making mud pies in a slum because he cannot imagine what is meant by the offer of a holiday at the sea" (1949, p. 26).*

Too often, we are unable to comprehend the "fullness of joy" to be found in God's presence and the "pleasures forevermore" at His right hand (Psalm 16:11). These things are what our souls truly crave, yet in our carnality, we instead covet what we think will bring us contentment. C.S. Lewis again writes, this time in *Mere Christianity*:

> *"All that we call human history—money, poverty, ambition, war, prostitution, classes, empires, slavery—[is] the long terrible story of man trying to find something other than God which will make him happy... God cannot give us a happiness and peace apart from Himself, because it is not there. There is no such thing" (1952, pp. 49-50).*

So, if you would be rid of covetousness and be filled with the sort of contentment that stanches cravings for increasing material riches and yet compels you to labor ever harder for the good of God's kingdom then:

> *"Seek the LORD while He may be found; call upon Him while He is near…For you shall go out in joy and be led forth in peace; the mountains and the hills before you shall break forth into singing, and all the trees of the fields shall clap their hands" (Isaiah 55:6, 12).*

Whatever provisions the Lord has planned for your business and your socioeconomic status, let it be enough! Of course, put forth your best efforts as you work diligently in your business, but be content with the level of wealth that God provides. If you are blessed with riches, do not allow them to consume you and be careful that you don't develop cravings for more and more. Instead, be thankful, be generous, and be content living beneath what you can afford.

While the balanced management of riches can be difficult, I have had the privilege of meeting quite a few highly respected, well-known Christian business leaders with substantial financial means who have succeeded in handling wealth in a God-honoring way. Many of those people made the decision to live in modest homes—one in particular in a modest condo. Their other spending choices have made it evident that their treasure is laid up in heaven and not here on earth, as Matthew 6:21 says, "For where your treasure is, there your heart will be also."

Where is your treasure? Is it in drywall, brick and mortar, land, cars, boats, motorcycles, business growth, or is your treasure in heaven? Are you sowing and reaping dollars and possessions or are you laboring to grow disciples of Christ? Is your treasure found in leading others to the Lord and helping believers to grow even closer to Him? Are you using your business to leave a legacy of souls reached for Christ, or a legacy of temporal things? Your heart will accompany your treasure store. You cannot serve both God and money, but given a right heart, you can serve God with the money that is generated through your business. Where is your heart? Does your heart covet temporal possessions or eternal rewards?

TAKE AWAY

- Coveting anything other than the things of God is a form of idolatry (Colossians 3:5), breaking both the first and second commandments.
- Coveting is a form of rebellion (Psalm 78:17-22).
- The antidote to coveting is contentment (Philippians 4:11-13, 19).
- For the covetous, enough is never enough (Ecclesiastes 5:10-11).
- Cultivate desires for eternal rewards rather than money or possessions (Matthew 6:21).

BONUS SCRIPTURE

# PROVERBS 22:7

*"The rich rules over the poor, and the borrower is the slave of the lender." —Proverbs 22:7*

(While this verse is not one of the Ten Commandments, its truth is so resonant that it arguably has as much bearing on business as the preceding verses shared in this volume.)

When we discuss the issue of debt, it is often easy to justify borrowing money since there is such a lack of understanding of what the Bible teaches regarding it. However, if we study the Scriptures with a heart that seeks to know God's mind and heart concerning debt, we will see that He actually has quite a lot to say on the subject. In fact, the Old Testament makes it clear that being debt-free is considered a sign of God's blessing and favor, while being bound in debt is conversely a manifestation of God's displeasure and judgment. Deuteronomy 28 says this regarding debt:

> *"And if you faithfully obey the voice of the Lord your God, being careful to do all his commandments that I command you today, the Lord your God will set you high above all the nations of the earth. And all these blessings shall come upon you and overtake you, if you obey the voice of the Lord your God... The Lord will open to you his good treasury, the heavens, to give the rain to your land in its season and to bless all the work of your hands.* ***And you shall lend to many nations, but you shall not borrow****... But if you will not obey the voice of the Lord your God or be careful to do all his commandments and his statutes that I command you today, then all these curses shall come upon you and overtake you...The sojourner who is among you shall rise higher and higher above you, and you shall come down lower and lower.* ***He shall lend to you, and you shall not lend to him****" (Deuteronomy 28:1-2, 12, 15, 43-44, emphasis added).*

Additionally, Romans 13:8 says quite simply, "Owe no one anything, except to love each other, for the one who loves another has fulfilled the law." Interesting, is it not, that the state of indebtedness toward others is juxtaposed here with an obligation to love others? If we ponder this idea, it becomes evident that to owe something to another *person* is to be under their constraint, either to pay them something or to do something for them. In contrast, the obligation we have to love others is *God's* constraint and calling upon us. It seems that, in wanting us to be free from debt, God is desiring us to be liberated from the constraints of the world and of other men. Instead He desires us to be subject to *Him alone*, rather than to both God and man, or even to man *above* God, as debt tempts us to do. As Matthew 6:24 warns, "No one can serve two masters, for either he will hate the one and love the other, or he will be devoted to the one and despise the other. You cannot serve God and money."

Further, God shows us the foolishness of taking on debt that we are not sure we will be able to repay. Indeed, debt—especially that which is taken on in order to run one's business—can actually become a slippery slope, since it seems more permissible than debt taken on for frivolous ends. Every day, business owners incur debt, which can only be repaid IF business goes as planned, but most deals seldom go exactly as planned. Proverbs 22:26-27 says this: "Be not one of those who give pledges, who put up security for debts. If you have nothing with which to pay, why should your bed be taken from under you?" You may have the best of intentions when you set up a payment plan, reckoning that you should definitely be able to pay what you owe, but there are many unforeseen circumstances that could transpire, and if you find yourself without the means to pay, you could lose everything. James 4:13-15 warns us of the frailty of human plans:

> *"Come now, you who say, 'Today or tomorrow we will go into such and such a town and spend a year there and trade and make a profit'—yet you do not know what tomorrow will bring. What is your life? For you are a mist that appears for a little time and then vanishes. Instead you ought to say, 'If the Lord wills, we will live and do this or that.'"*

We must be careful that what we borrow, we are able to repay without depending upon our businesses being as successful as we predict that they will be, else we may risk losing everything if our anticipated circumstances change.

While many small business owners relish in the autonomy that being one's own boss can afford, they too often fail to understand that when they are in debt to someone else, they are no longer working for themselves but for their creditors. After all, they make daily decisions based upon strategies meant to please and recompense those to whom they are indebted. In short, the creditors call the shots and their debtors have no choice but to accept those terms, whatever they may be.

Debt can enslave small business owners in a couple of key ways. First, it can bind them spiritually, mentally, and emotionally. Debt—especially when it is a crushing amount, will almost certainly become your primary focus in life. You will wake up thinking about it, you will go to sleep thinking about it, and it will trouble the majority of your thoughts between those two times. Since the debt, rather than God, has become the focal point of your life and your actions, it has undeniably become an unwanted idol that has the potential to crush not only your business, but your soul as well. A preoccupation with repaying one's debtors renders you incapable of prioritizing God's will and plan for your life because the bills that are constantly before you have a singular way of capturing your immediate focus and attention.

The crushing load of debt is a reality that I have experienced firsthand throughout my life. Growing up, my father was a farmer in rural North Carolina. Like many other farmers in our area, he experienced several bad years in a row, leaving him unable to repay the massive amount of debt that the farm had taken on to support itself. It all came to a head when I was fourteen. Our family farm, all of the farm equipment, and even our home were sold at auction to settle everything we owed. We had to start over in a new place with little more than the clothes on our backs. Later on, at the end of my first year in business, I was in a deep hole of debt, both business and personal. Thankfully, due to the blessing of the Lord, a lot of hard work, and disciplined spending; I found myself debt-free four years later, with the exception of the mortgage on my home. Those four years were intensely stressful—every decision was made based upon getting the mountain of debt ameliorated as quickly as possible. The tension created from the debt was also intensified with the responsibilities of being newly married and having two small children. So, as you can see, I am very familiar with the struggle of dealing with an overwhelming amount of debt and the level of stress and pain that it can cause.

Debt can also enslave you by preventing you from being financially free to give to the work of the Lord, or to others in need. Giving to others is something that we are commanded to do and is a mark of those truly in Christ, as Matthew 25 indicates:

> *"Then the King will say to those on his right, 'Come, you who are blessed by my Father, inherit the kingdom prepared for you from the foundation of the world. For I was hungry and you gave me food, I was thirsty and you gave me drink, I was a stranger and you welcomed me, I was naked and you clothed me, I was sick and you visited me, I was in prison and you came to me... Truly, I say to you, as you did it to one of the least of these my brothers, you did it to me'" (verses 34-36, 40).*

When we are held in the bondage of debt, our funds are often not free to be used as we will, as any extra money we have must be put toward the payment of what is owed. One of the great joys of Christian living is the pleasure that comes from helping others in the name of Jesus. Under a crippling load of debt, our ability to give to others is severely limited and thus we miss out on those opportunities to help others and the joy that would have followed.

As we explore the issue of bondage as it relates to business debt, there are a couple of examples that come to my mind. In my years of accounting, I have had two separate clients that operate in identical industries and have businesses of similar size. Client A operates debt-free. All his equipment is purchased with cash, his personal spending is reasonable, and he saves and invests his excess cash—even his real estate is owned free of debt. This client is financially free and he is able to give generously to his church as well as to others that have genuine needs.

In contrast, Client B is drowning in debt. All of his equipment is financed, his personal spending is beyond what he can afford, and there is no excess cash for saving or investing. Further, since there is no money to pay income taxes, he usually increases his equipment debt each year to avoid owing tax. Client B can barely afford to make ends meet, much less to give generously to help others. In fact, his bondage is so great, that he cannot even sell the business at fair market value, since the value of the business is less than the debt on the property and the income tax obligations. He recently had to turn down a business purchase offer of one million dollars because he would have been required to bring $150,000 to the bargaining table to close the deal! Client B is in bondage to such a great degree that he would actually have to pay to sell his business.

Which of these two clients would you imagine is experiencing joy as a Christian business owner? Which of them would be prepared to weather a downturn in business? Which of these clients are you more like? Obviously, being debt-free, like Client A, is a great goal for all Christian business owners. Unfortunately, I see many believers in business who are bound up in debt, like Client B. 1 Corinthians 7:23 makes it clear to us, however, that the Lord's desire for us is that we not be in bondage!

Let's look at some practical ways to help limit your debt to a manageable amount. One of the best ways is to establish specific criteria that must be met before you agree to take on new obligations. According to *Discovering God's Way of Handling Your Money*, a Bible study published by Crown Financial Ministries, there are two sets of three criteria that potential debt must meet in order to be considered "permissible" (course workbook, 1999, p. 17). The first set of three criteria shared in the study, posit that debt can only be justified if it is undertaken for your "(1) home mortgage, (2) your vocation or (3) your business" (1999, p. 17). If the proposed debt falls under one of these three categories, then the second set of three specifications (included as follows) can be used to sift between appropriate and exorbitant debt: "1. The item purchased produces an income or has the potential to appreciate. 2. The value of the item equals or exceeds the amount owed against it. 3. The debt is not so high that the repayment puts undue strain on the budget" (*Discovering God's Way of Handling Money*, course workbook, 1999, p. 17). Let's break these criteria down a bit more in order to give a better understanding of what is meant by this list.

First, an item that "produces an income or has the potential to appreciate" can apply to a house or other type of building, or a piece of machinery or other investment that can generate capital in order to repay the debt owed, or that retains or increases its value in such a way that it could be sold in order to cancel the debt (*Discovering God's Way of Handling Your Money* course workbook, 1999, p. 17). If the item generates revenue, then it is able to pay for itself, preventing stress from making payments on an existing budget. Additionally, if the item appreciates, it has the potential to end the debt entirely if it were to be sold. Either way, there is a clear path out of debt for you, even if circumstances take a turn in an unanticipated direction. The same principle applies to an item with a value that "equals or exceeds the amount owed against it" (*Discovering God's Way of Handling Your Money* course workbook, 1999, p. 17). It is able to be sold to escape the debt, if for any reason it becomes too burdensome.

The final criterion—that the debt be "not so high that the repayment puts undue strain on the budget"—is meant to preserve your financial freedom and peace of mind, both with regard to God and to man (*Discovering God's Way of Handling Your Money* course workbook, 1999, p. 17). If, taking into account all of your currently held cash, assets, amounts payable and receivable, and your current liabilities; you find that the purchase of the desired item should be an affordable and profitable investment that will be easily repaid through a dependable and sufficient revenue stream, then it may be justifiable. However, if the debt will be stressful for you to repay, causing you to constantly worry from month to month, hoping that the needed funds will continue to be available on time to repay your creditor, then the loan is simply not worth it.

No *item* is worth enslaving you, body, mind, and soul. If a purchase proposition does not meet the outlined requirements, let it pass by you without a single regret. You can trust the Lord to provide for your needs; as the Scripture says, "For all the nations of the world seek after these things [physical needs], and your Father knows that you need them" (Luke 12:30). He "will supply every need of yours according to his riches in glory in Christ Jesus" (Philippians 4:19). **Do not feel that you must take on burdensome and unbiblical debt in order to run the business that God has called you to lead**. As the missionary, James Hudson Taylor, said, "God's work done in God's way will never lack God's supplies" (Lyall, 1965, p. 37).

Keep in mind: debt itself is not a sin. However, in Scripture it is frequently discouraged and portrayed negatively. Used with restraint, some manageable debt may be beneficial. But used in excess, debt can absolutely destroy your business and your joy. Resist bondage, resist debt, and live with the freedom and joy the Lord intends for you.

TAKE AWAY

- Debt creates financial, emotional, and spiritual bondage.
- Debt impedes your ability to receive joy by serving and giving to others.
- A managed level of debt with a sure way to repay may be appropriate (see the criteria in the chapter).
- Living without debt gives you freedom and can greatly increase your joy and peace.

# CONCLUSION

*"But seek first the kingdom of God and his righteousness, and all these things will be added to you." —Matthew 6:33*

*"Go therefore and make disciples of all nations, baptizing them in the name of the Father and of the Son and of the Holy Spirit." —Matthew 28:19*

You've reached the conclusion of this book, and I want to encourage you as you go forth on your journey throughout life and business to continue to seek God's glory and the furtherance of His kingdom above all else. As a Christian business owner myself, and as one who has many Christian business owners in my acquaintance, I know how much each of us desires that our business be better tomorrow than it is today. In fact, that ambitious desire forms part of the core character of an entrepreneur. It's not necessarily a bad thing—in a way, that desire is what gives us motivation to persevere when things become challenging. Ambition itself is not wrong, but we must always ask ourselves this question: What is the object of my ambition? Is your ambition to attain the riches and power that the world equates with success, or is it your ambition to grow in the righteousness of God and to make more disciples for Christ?

My proposition to you is this: if you will embrace the application of the Ten Commandments for your business, as well as all the other business wisdom found in Scripture, then your business will able to perform at its best, which will permit you the time, freedom, and resources to fervently pursue Christ yourself and to lead others to Him.

In reality, we do not have to choose to succeed either exclusively as a business owner or as a believer. The truth is that if we apply the principles of Scripture to our businesses, then we are poised to be simultaneously successful both as a business owner and as a Christian. Our businesses become our platforms for pursuing righteousness and for making disciples.

*The Ten Commandments for Business* is just the tip of the iceberg. There is so much more biblical business wisdom that is freely available to you in the pages of God's Holy Word. My challenge to every business owner is this: dig deeply into the Word of the Lord, mining the Scriptures for business wisdom and application. Look for it as you would look for gold, and the Lord will reveal to you all the wisdom you need to achieve everything that He has ordained for you.

Let this reminder of the importance of the Word of God be on our minds continually:

> *"My son, be attentive to my words; incline your ear to my sayings. Let them not escape from your sight; keep them within your heart. For they are life to those who find them, and healing to all their flesh" (Proverbs 4:20-22).*

May the Word of the Lord bring life and healing for you and your business!

# About
# The Word on Business

The Word on Business exists to help small-business owners apply biblical principles to their businesses to overcome stress, frustration, and ineffectiveness and to help them glorify God with their work.

Our vision is to see Christian business owners grow in their faith as they grow in the application of God's Holy Word to their enterprise, resulting in businesses that can maximize their witness for the kingdom of God.

Our mission is to equip and encourage followers of Christ to apply biblical wisdom to their businesses, so that time and funds may be set at liberty to be used for witnessing to others and for God's glory.

To learn more about how TWOB can help you accomplish God's will for you and your business through our Inner-Circle membership, our Biblical Business Boot Camp, or other available resources, please visit our website at TheWordonBusiness.com. Or you can contact us at adam@thewordonbusiness.com. We look forward to serving you!

# ABOUT *the* AUTHOR

Adam Hall founded The Word on Business (TWOB) with one goal in mind: to use his own experience of bondage and deliverance in business to help other Christian business owners experience freedom for the purpose of maximizing their eternal impact for the kingdom of God. In 1994, at the age of 22, he began his own accounting firm with just 5 clients, and by 2000, the practice had exploded to serve over 1,300 clients. The success came at the cost of Adam's spiritual and physical health, which became apparent when his health insurance company declared him uninsurable—at the tender age of 28!

It was at this point that Adam realized a life-changing truth—that his business was meant for an eternal purpose that could never be fulfilled under the existing operating conditions. In order for the practice to glorify God and to allow Adam to fulfill his calling to make disciples and to be an attentive husband and father, something would need to change. Through extensive prayer and study, Adam experienced the Lord's deliverance from bondage to his business by implementing business management principles that are evident in the Bible.

Once the practice was re-engineered to run in accordance with biblical wisdom, it no longer proved a hindrance to Adam's relationships with God and with his family, and his health was able to improve. Rather than being a burden, the practice instead became a conduit of blessing and ministry. This experience was the inspiration for creating TWOB, an organization that teaches biblical business principles to help Christian business owners achieve their best for Christ through their work.

Adam graduated *summa cum laude* from Methodist University with a B.S. in accounting and a minor in music. He is a CPA, as well as a certified Chartered Global Management Accountant (CGMA). Adam and his wife, Terrah, live in North Carolina, have been married for 22 years, and are thankful for the blessing of 10 lovely children.

# REFERENCES


## Introduction

- Guinness World Records Ltd,. (n.d.). Retrieved February 15, 2018, from www.guinnessworldrecords.com/world-records/best-selling-book-of-non-fiction/
- Crossway Bibles. (2007). *ESV: study Bible: English Standard Version*. Wheaton, Ill: Crossway Bibles.

## Commandment 3

- Erlick, R. A. (2017, July 19). Respecting the name of God. Retrieved January 25, 2018, from www.jewishjournal.com/culture/religion/torah_portion/218961/respecting-name-god/
- Henry, M. (1706). *Exodus 20*. In *Matthew Henry commentary on the whole Bible (complete)*. Retrieved from

www.biblestudytools.com/commentaries/matthew-henry-complete/exodus/20.html.

## Commandment 4

- Bartiromo, M. (2017, December 18). Chick-fil-A opens on Sunday, provides food to stranded passengers at Atlanta airport. Retrieved February 13, 2018, from www.foxnews.com/food-drink/2017/12/18/chick-fil-opens-on-sunday-provides-food-to-stranded-passengers-at-atlanta-airport.html
- Peterson, H. (2017, August 01). Why Chick-fil-A's restaurants sell 4 times as much as KFC's. Retrieved February 16, 2018, from www.businessinsider.com/why-chick-fil-a-is-so-successful-2017-8

## Commandment 6

- Lewis, C.S. (1949). *The Weight of Glory: And Other Addresses*. New York, NY: HarperCollins Publishers.

## Commandment 7

- Blake, A. (2017, March 30). Mike Pence doesn't dine alone with other women. And we're all shocked. Retrieved

January 25, 2018, from www.washingtonpost.com/news/the-fix/wp/2017/03/30/mike-pence-doesnt-dine-alone-with-other-women-and-were-all-shocked/

- Porn Use Increases Infidelity, Divorce. (2010, April 02). Retrieved February 15, 2018, from www.marriagegems.com/2010/04/02/porn-use-increases-infidelity-divorce/
- DeHaas, R. (2016, January 19). What are the most up-to-date stats on porn? Retrieved February 15, 2018, from www.covenanteyes.com/2016/01/19/what-are-the-most-up-to-date-stats-on-pornography/

**Commandment 8**

- Deffinbaugh, R. L. (2004, May 13). The Sin of Stealing (Exodus 20:15). Retrieved April 17, 2017, from www.bible.org/seriespage/21-sin-stealing-exodus-2015

**Commandment 9**

- Sumner, S. (2011, May 20). The Seven Levels of Lying. Retrieved January 25, 2018, from www.christianitytoday.com/ct/2011/may/7-levelslying.html
- Ten Boom, C. (1971). *The Hiding Place.* New York, NY: Bantam Books.

**Commandment 10**

- Lewis, C.S. (1949). *The Weight of Glory: And Other Addresses.* New York, NY: HarperCollins Publishers.
- Lewis, C.S. (1952). *Mere Christianity.* New York, NY: HarperCollins Publishers.

**Bonus Verse**

- *Discovering God's Way of Handling Your Money* [Course Workbook, pp. 16-18]. (1999). Gainesville, GA: Crown Financial Ministries, Inc.
- Lyall, L.T. (1965). *A Passion for the Impossible: The Continuing Story of the Mission Hudson Taylor Began.* London: OMF Books.

# ENDORSEMENTS

*"This is very powerful! I enjoyed every word and can really see this book helping many small business owners. This is very needed. Excellent book!"* —Handre De Jongh, Crown Financial Ministries, Vice President, Global Outreach

*"Adam Hall has done us all a favor by structuring his book after the Ten Commandments. In doing so, he is proclaiming the absolute sufficiency and applicability of the Bible. He draws from his many years of personal experience and connects that experience with the Word of God, proving that God is true, and that you can trust Him by obeying Him in every aspect of your business. I've never seen a book like this that so explicitly explains the Ten Commandments to prepare us for a life of business."*
—Scott Brown, President, National Center for Family-Integrated Churches

*"A must have for every business owner! A biblical, motivational, and easy-to-read book with practical tips to help align your new or existing business with the Word of God...."*
—Jennifer Massey, DDS, President, Seven Lakes Family Dentistry

*"Awesome! For those wanting to check for blind spots in the way that they honor God in the business they manage, or for those who are new to business or the faith, this is an indispensable resource. Great real life examples and practical steps ready for use. You will be blessed simply by reading; everyone around you will be blessed by your implementation."*
—Art McKee, President, McKee Investment Planning

*"Just as adhering to the principles of the Ten Commandments makes everyone a better citizen, adhering to the Ten Commandments for Business can make every manager better and can help the businesses they manage become more profitable."*
—Dan Hayes, President, Stedman Drug Center and Eastover Drug

*"In reading and meditating on the words within I was filled with the spirit of truth and integrity that we all must possess in order to fully receive God's true blessings. I strongly urge all Christians and every business leader to practice what it preaches."*
—Tommy Honeycutt, President, Tolar Supply Company

*"The wisdom contained in this book is as timeless as the Bible it is based on and will provide a path for building a Christian culture in your business in the midst of a secular world. What a blessing to see a business book with an eternal perspective!"*
—Jim Doherty, Area Chair, C12 Group

*"This book is brilliant in its simplicity. It is as true as the time-tested principles it is based upon. Who would have thought there was so much practical wisdom for modern-day business owners in Moses' Decalogue? I highly recommend this gem of a resource. It may very well be used by God to change the lives of countless people within your sphere of influence, beginning with you and your household."*
—Joaquin Fernandez, Producer, Great Commission Films

*"Brilliant book filled with insights about applying God's word to business. It is clear that Hall has thought through this subject deeply. Read this book and find yourself challenged and encouraged to apply biblical ethics in the workplace. This should be required reading for every young Christian in business school."*
—Bob Allen, Jr., President, D. R. Allen & Son, Inc.